2025
VISION
BOARD

2in1 CLIP ART BOOK
& Essentials Guide

FOR WOMEN

Contact us with any questions

Your Free Gifts

Thank you for purchasing our book!
Below, you'll find a link to download your valuable bonuses.
Created with love, these resources are designed to enrich
your journey, making it even more efficient and joyful.

1

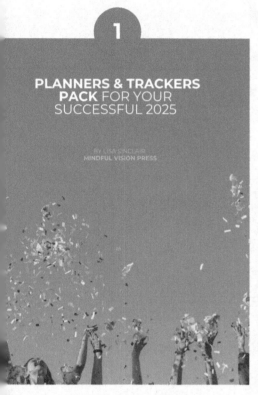

PLANNERS & TRACKERS
PACK FOR YOUR
SUCCESSFUL 2025

BY LISA SINCLAIR
MINDFUL VISION PRESS

2

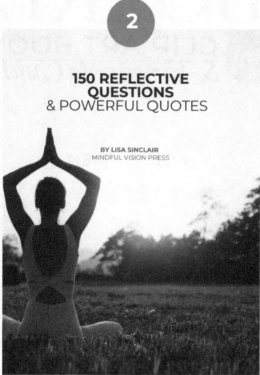

150 REFLECTIVE
QUESTIONS
& POWERFUL QUOTES

BY LISA SINCLAIR
MINDFUL VISION PRESS

3

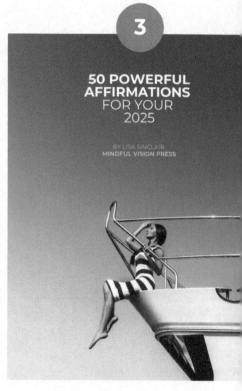

50 POWERFUL
AFFIRMATIONS
FOR YOUR
2025

BY LISA SINCLAIR
MINDFUL VISION PRESS

Pack of **Essential Planners for your Manifestation Journey,** including Goals, Gratitude, Habits & Self-Care (Printable PDF)

All the **150 Thoughtful Reflective Questions & Insightful Quotes** that you find through the pages of this Book (Printable PDF)

50 Powerful, Motivational **Affirmations** to enhance inspiration and make **Your 2025 The Best Year** (Printable PDF)

Just scan it.
We wish you blissful, effortless, and successful
Dream Manifestation!

WHATEVER
YOU CAN DO, OR DREAM
YOU CAN, BEGIN IT,
BOLDNESS HAS GENIUS,
POWER AND MAGIC IN IT

don't be afraid to fail
be afraid not to try

DREAM MORE

12 New Chapters 365 New Chances

YOU BECOME
WHAT YOU
BELIEVE.

2025

NOW OR NEVER

REFLECTIVE QUESTIONS
New Year Goals

1

WHAT ARE THE TOP THREE AREAS OF MY LIFE THAT I WANT TO IMPROVE OR FOCUS ON (E.G., CAREER, HEALTH, RELATIONSHIPS)?

2

WHAT SPECIFIC GOALS DO I WANT TO ACHIEVE IN THE NEXT YEAR?

3

WHAT IS ONE MAJOR ACHIEVEMENT I WANT TO MANIFEST IN THE NEXT 3 YEARS?

4

WHAT DOES SUCCESS MEAN TO ME PERSONALLY, AND HOW CAN I REFLECT THAT DEFINITION ON MY VISION BOARD AND WITHIN MY GOALS?

5

WHAT DOES HAPPINESS TRULY MEAN FOR ME, AND HOW CAN I CREATE MORE OF IT IN MY EVERYDAY LIFE?

All the questions are available in a separate bonus file (link provided at the beginning of the book). So, no worries about cutting!

The Power
OF VISUALIZATION

Visualization is one of the most powerful tools you can use to turn your dreams into reality. By creating a clear and vivid picture of your goals, you send a message to your Mind and to the Universe that your desires are not just wishes but achievable realities.

When you visualize your future, you're not just thinking about what you want—you're programming your brain to stay focused, take action, and attract the right opportunities.

IF YOU CAN DREAM IT
YOU CAN DO IT.

– WALT DISNEY

5 Principles
OF WORKING WITH VISION

Clarity of Intent

Clearly define your dreams and goals before creating your board. Know what you want to attract into your life.

Visual Inspiration

Use for your board images, words, and symbols that inspire and resonate with your desires, spark joy and excitement.

Emmotional Connection

Fully immerse yourself in the feeling of already achieving your desire. The more realistic this feeling is, the more strongly you align yourself with success.

Consistency

Keep your vision board in a place where you can see it daily, reminding yourself of your goals and maintaining focus, building deeper emotional connection every day.

Action and Belief

Pair your vision with practical steps, while maintaining belief in your capacity to achieve your dreams.

1. Clarity

OF INTENT

If you need to define your dreams and specific goals,
you can use these tools:

1. WHEEL OF LIFE

Use this tool to get
a comprehensive overview
of your life.
Find the instruction below.

2. REFLECTIVE QUESTIONS

Explore reflective questions
that dive deeper into each
life sphere. You'll find them
on the pages opposite
the images for each area.

THE WHEEL OF LIFE. HOW TO USE IT?

1. **Identify the Key Life Spheres:**
   You can use predefined categories
   or customize them to fit your
   own priorities.

2. **Rate Each Sphere:** On a scale of 1 to 10,
   rate your current level of fulfillment in each
   area. Be honest with yourself—this
   assessment is meant to reflect where you
   feel you are now, not where you wish to be.

3. **Connect the Dots around the wheel:**
   This will give you a visual representation
   of the balance (or imbalance) in your life.

WHEEL OF LIFE

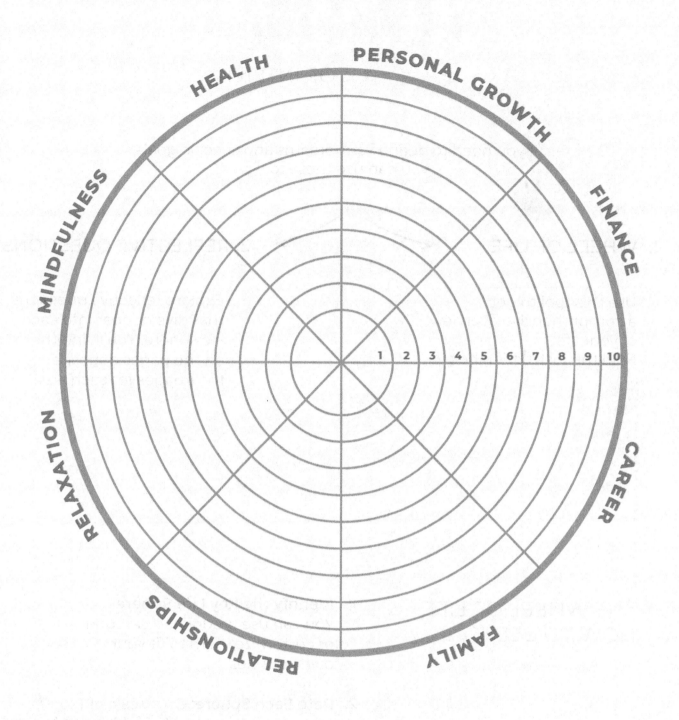

Ask yourself:

Which areas are lacking?
Which areas are thriving?
Which areas will I focus on
this year?

PRIORITY AREAS

2.Visual
INSPIRATION

Choose images, words, and symbols for your board that truly inspire you and reflect your deepest desires. Let them come from your heart, not from what others think you should want.

TO UNDERSTAND
THIS, ASK YOURSELF:

"Does this make me feel truly excited and aligned with my dreams, or am I choosing it because of external influences?"

FOLLOW

YOUR

HEART

3. Emotional
CONNECTION

Emotional connection is the key element that sets effective visualization apart from mere positive thinking.

You need to truly feel the achievement you desire, as if it's already happening in your life for real. The deeper your emotional connection, the more powerfully you align with success. In other words, you're "tuning into the right frequency"— and that's exactly what we aim for.

Try the **'Future Self Visualization'** practice, which is highly effective.
Set aside 3-5 minutes in the morning, ideally at least three times a week. Close your eyes, take several deep breaths, and imagine yourself already living the life you desire.
Let your emotions flow as though you've already achieved your goal.

Visualize every detail—what you see, feel, hear, and experience. The key is to immerse yourself in the joy, pride, and excitement of your success, as if it's happening right now. Goosebumps!

4. Consistency

Are you more of a bedroom person or a living room person?
Do you feel comfortable sharing your dreams with others,
or do you prefer to keep them private?
Would you rather display your vision on a big board
or keep it in a cozy A4 notebook?

Whatever your style, the key is to place your vision board where you
can see it daily. It's all about keeping your goals front and center,
helping you stay focused. Whether it's on your nightstand in
the bedroom or on a big wall in the living room, having your vision
board visible will strengthen your emotional connection to your
dreams day by day.

YOU SEE IT, YOU FEEL IT, YOU LIVE IT.

5. Action

& BELIEF

And now it's time to pair your perfect visualization job with real, actionable steps.

The good news is that once you're truly inspired and clear about your wishes, taking action becomes easier. And more you are emotionally connected "living" your dream life in your head and in your heart as if it's really happening—more the Universe will support you by providing signs and events that will guide and help you on the way.

These signs and events may seem to be 'magical coincidences'.. but they are not. Actually it's the result of your strong vision aligning with the "frequency of the Universe" as they may say.. whatever words we use, main outcome is the opening of the clear path towards the realization of your dreams.

TIP: Celebrate small wins along the way, as this will keep you motivated and boost your confidence as you progress toward your larger goals. Be grateful and compassionate to yourself!

BIG JOURNEYS BEGIN
WITH SMALL STEPS

3 Secrets
TO SUCCESS

And before you begin creating your magical vision board,
I'd love to share with you three additional tips that are always
helping a lot along the way.

1. GRATEFUL HEART

As you focus on your future, it's essential to be
grateful for what you already have in your life.
Gratitude keeps you grounded and amplifies positive
energy.

2. FOCUS

Focus on a couple of areas at a time rather
than trying to improve everything at once.

3. TRUST THE PROCESS

Obsessing over your desires can create fear and block
progress. Keep visualizing and taking action but trust
the process—things will unfold naturally and in their
own time.

Your vision board is not just a collection of dreams—
it's a roadmap to your future.

Every image, every word is a reminder that you have
the power to manifest the life you desire.

Believe in your vision, take inspired action, and watch
as your dreams unfold into reality.

I CAN AND I WILL

Watch me.

2025 VISION BOARD

HAPPY NEW YEAR

COLD *Nights* WARM *Lights*

THIS WILL BE A *good year*

Past Year & New Year

1
WHAT BROUGHT ME THE MOST JOY AND FULFILLMENT
THIS YEAR AND HOW CAN I CREATE MORE OF THOSE MOMENTS
IN THE NEW ONE?

2
WHAT CHALLENGES DID I FACE AND HOW
DID I OVERCOME THEM?

3
HOW DID I GROW PERSONALLY OVER THE PAST YEAR
AND WHAT LESSONS DID I LEARN?

4
HOW DID I VIEW MYSELF THROUGHOUT THE YEAR,
AND IN WHAT WAYS DID MY SELF-PERCEPTION CHANGE?

5
LOOKING BACK OVER THE PAST YEAR, DID I FEEL HAPPY
AND FULFILLED? WHAT BROUGHT ME THIS FEELING,
AND HOW CAN I CARRY MORE OF IT INTO THE YEAR AHEAD?

All the questions are available in a separate bonus file (link provided at the beginning of the book). So, no worries about cutting!

Believe something wonderful to happen

SUCCESS

NEW YEAR
NEW ME

Dream Big

2025

YOU ARE
THE
MAGIC

This is my YEAR TO sparkle

REFLECTIVE QUESTIONS
Love Relationships & Family

1
WHAT KIND OF RELATIONSHIP OR FAMILY DYNAMIC DO I ENVISION FOR MYSELF, AND WHAT STEPS CAN I TAKE TO ALIGN MY CURRENT LIFE WITH THAT VISION?

2
HOW DO I WANT TO FEEL IN MY ROMANTIC RELATIONSHIPS OR WITHIN MY FAMILY, AND WHAT CHANGES CAN I MAKE TO ACHIEVE THAT EMOTIONAL STATE?

3
WHAT SPECIFIC GOALS DO I HAVE FOR MY RELATIONSHIPS (E.G., DEEPER CONNECTION, BETTER COMMUNICATION, STARTING A FAMILY)?

4
IN WHAT WAYS CAN I BE MORE PRESENT AND SUPPORTIVE FOR MY LOVED ONES, AND HOW CAN THIS BE A PART OF MY LONG-TERM VISION FOR A HARMONIOUS FAMILY LIFE?

5
WHAT POSITIVE CHANGES DO I WANT TO BRING INTO MY FAMILY LIFE OVER THE NEXT YEAR?

All the questions are available in a separate bonus file (link provided at the beginning of the book). So, no worries about cutting!

"They say love is the best investment;
the more you give, the more you get in return."
— Audrey Hepburn

"Never above you. Never below you. Always beside you."
— Walter Winchell

My Family

"Family : A little bit of crazy, a little bit of loud, and a whole lot of love."

— Unknown

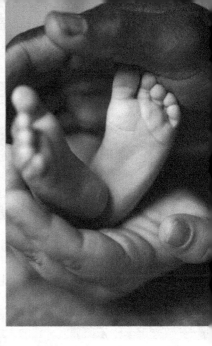

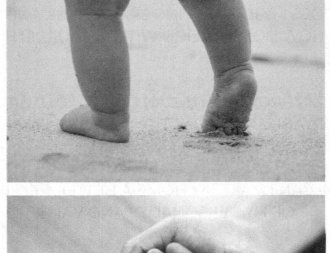

REFLECTIVE QUESTIONS

My Ideal Home

1
WHAT DOES MY IDEAL LIVING SPACE LOOK AND FEEL LIKE,
AND HOW DOES IT ALIGN WITH MY CURRENT HOME?

2
WHAT CHANGES OR IMPROVEMENTS CAN I MAKE TO CREATE A MORE PEACEFUL,
COMFORTABLE, AND FUNCTIONAL HOME ENVIRONMENT?

3
HOW CAN I MAKE MY HOME A BETTER REFLECTION
OF MY PERSONALITY AND VALUES?

4
WHAT AREAS OF MY HOME DO I WANT TO ORGANIZE OR DECLUTTER,
AND HOW WOULD THAT IMPROVE MY WELL-BEING?

5
HOW CAN I CREATE SPACES IN MY HOME THAT INSPIRE CREATIVITY, RELAXATION,
OR PRODUCTIVITY?

6
WHAT LONG-TERM GOALS DO I HAVE FOR MY LIVING SITUATION,
SUCH AS BUYING A HOME, MOVING TO A DIFFERENT LOCATION,
OR RENOVATING, AND HOW CAN I START WORKING
TOWARD THOSE DREAMS?

All the questions are available in a separate bonus file (link provided at the beginning of the book). So, no worries about cutting!

HOME
SWEET
HOME

"Home is where you can make a mess
and not get in trouble."
— John le Carré

"Maybe that's the best part of going away
for a vacation—is coming home again."
— Madeleine L'Engle

Friendship & Social Relationships

1

WHAT QUALITIES DO I VALUE MOST IN MY FRIENDSHIPS,
AND HOW CAN I NURTURE THOSE QUALITIES IN MY CURRENT RELATIONSHIPS?

2

HOW DO I WANT TO FEEL IN MY SOCIAL INTERACTIONS,
AND WHAT CAN I DO TO CREATE MORE OF THOSE POSITIVE FEELINGS?

3

ARE THERE FRIENDSHIPS IN MY LIFE THAT I NEED TO INVEST MORE TIME
AND ENERGY INTO?

4

ARE THERE ANY SOCIAL RELATIONSHIPS THAT DRAIN MY ENERGY
OR NO LONGER ALIGN WITH MY VALUES?

5

WHAT TYPE OF NEW FRIENDSHIPS OR CONNECTIONS DO I WANT TO ATTRACT
INTO MY LIFE?

6

HOW CAN I BE MORE PRESENT AND SUPPORTIVE IN MY CURRENT SOCIAL CIRCLE?

7

WHAT ROLE DO I PLAY IN MY FRIENDSHIPS, AND HOW DO I WANT TO GROW
IN THAT ROLE?

8

IN WHAT WAYS CAN I IMPROVE MY COMMUNICATION WITH FRIENDS
TO STRENGTHEN OUR BOND?

9

HOW DO I BALANCE TIME SPENT WITH FRIENDS, FAMILY, AND PERSONAL TIME,
AND WHAT CHANGES WOULD I LIKE TO MAKE?

10

WHAT ACTIVITIES OR EXPERIENCES DO I WANT TO SHARE WITH MY FRIENDS
TO DEEPEN OUR CONNECTION?

All the questions are available in a separate bonus file (link provided at the beginning of the book). So, no worries about cutting!

GOOD TIMES + CRAZY FRIENDS = AMAZING MEMORIES

REFLECTIVE QUESTIONS
Health & Fitness

1
WHAT AREAS OF MY HEALTH NEED THE MOST ATTENTION RIGHT NOW?

2
HOW DO I WANT TO FEEL PHYSICALLY AND MENTALLY IN THE NEXT YEAR, AND WHAT STEPS CAN I TAKE TO ACHIEVE THAT?

3
HOW DO I CURRENTLY FEEL ABOUT MY ENERGY LEVELS, AND WHAT IMPROVEMENTS WOULD I LIKE TO SEE?

4
WHAT SPECIFIC FITNESS GOALS DO I WANT TO ACHIEVE IN THE NEXT SIX MONTHS (E.G., STRENGTH, FLEXIBILITY, WEIGHT LOSS), AND HOW WILL I TRACK MY PROGRESS?

5
WHAT FITNESS ACTIVITIES DO I ENJOY, AND HOW CAN I INCORPORATE THEM MORE REGULARLY INTO MY LIFE?

6
HOW CAN I CREATE A BALANCED ROUTINE THAT SUPPORTS BOTH PHYSICAL AND MENTAL WELL-BEING?

7
HOW CAN I OVERCOME EXCUSES OR OBSTACLES THAT PREVENT ME FROM PRIORITIZING FITNESS?

8
HOW CAN I INCORPORATE MORE MOVEMENT AND EXERCISE INTO MY DAILY ROUTINE?

9
WHAT BARRIERS ARE CURRENTLY HOLDING ME BACK FROM BETTER HEALTH, AND HOW CAN I OVERCOME THEM?

10
WHAT HABITS CONTRIBUTE POSITIVELY TO MY HEALTH, AND HOW CAN I STRENGTHEN THEM?

All the questions are available in a separate bonus file (link provided at the beginning of the book). So, no worries about cutting!

MY
SUMMER
BODY
IS IN
PROGRESS

TIME
to lose
WEIGHT

love your
body because
it's yours

REFLECTIVE QUESTIONS
Food Habits

1

HOW DO I CURRENTLY FEEL ABOUT MY OVERALL EATING HABITS?

2

WHAT ROLE DOES FOOD PLAY IN MY DAILY LIFE—FUEL, COMFORT,
OR STRESS RELIEF?

3

AM I MAKING INTENTIONAL FOOD CHOICES, OR DO I TEND
TO EAT OUT OF CONVENIENCE?

4

HOW OFTEN DO I PREPARE MEALS AT HOME, AND HOW DOES THIS IMPACT
MY NUTRITION?

5

AM I CONSUMING A BALANCED VARIETY OF NUTRIENTS,
INCLUDING PROTEINS, CARBS, AND FATS?

6

DO I DRINK ENOUGH WATER DAILY, AND HOW CAN I IMPROVE
MY HYDRATION HABITS?

7

HOW FREQUENTLY DO I EAT PROCESSED FOODS,
AND HOW CAN I REDUCE THEM?

8

DO I CONSUME ENOUGH FIBER, VITAMINS, AND MINERALS
THROUGH FRUITS AND VEGETABLES?

9

HOW DO MY FOOD CHOICES CONTRIBUTE TO MY OVERALL SENSE
OF JOY AND HAPPINESS?

10

HOW CAN I FOSTER MEANINGFUL FAMILY MOMENTS BY SHARING
HEALTHY MEALS TOGETHER MORE OFTEN?

All the questions are available in a separate bonus file (link provided at the beginning of the book). So, no worries about cutting!

eat
~~less~~
BETTER

IS
GOOD
MOOD

NO
SUGAR

REFLECTIVE QUESTIONS
Me & Sports

1

HOW DO I FEEL ABOUT MY CURRENT LEVEL OF PARTICIPATION
IN SPORTS, AND DOES IT ALIGN WITH MY FITNESS GOALS?

2

WHAT SPORTS OR PHYSICAL ACTIVITIES BRING ME THE MOST JOY
AND MOTIVATION TO STAY ACTIVE?

3

DO I APPROACH SPORTS AS A WAY TO IMPROVE MY HEALTH,
OR DO I FEEL PRESSURED TO COMPETE OR PERFORM?

4

HOW CAN I BETTER BALANCE SPORTS WITH OTHER ASPECTS
OF MY LIFE TO MAINTAIN A HEALTHY ROUTINE?

5

WHAT STEPS CAN I TAKE TO DEEPEN MY ENGAGEMENT WITH SPORTS
AND MAKE IT A MORE FULFILLING PART OF MY LIFE?

All the questions are available in a separate bonus file (link provided at the beginning of the book). So, no worries about cutting!

212

YES
YOU
CAN

REFLECTIVE QUESTIONS
My Hobbies

1
WHAT HOBBIES BRING ME THE MOST JOY AND FULFILLMENT?

2
HOW OFTEN DO I MAKE TIME FOR ACTIVITIES I TRULY ENJOY?
ARE THERE ANY HOBBIES I'VE NEGLECTED THAT I WANT TO RECONNECT WITH?

3
WHAT NEW SKILLS OR HOBBIES WOULD I LIKE TO EXPLORE?

4
DO I FEEL A SENSE OF GROWTH OR ACCOMPLISHMENT THROUGH MY HOBBIES?

5
WHAT HOBBIES HELP ME RELAX AND RECHARGE?

6
AM I PURSUING HOBBIES JUST FOR FUN, OR DO I FEEL PRESSURED
TO BE PRODUCTIVE?

7
HOW CAN I BALANCE MY HOBBIES WITH OTHER RESPONSIBILITIES?

8
WHICH HOBBIES ALLOW ME TO EXPRESS MY CREATIVITY OR PASSIONS?

9
HOW CAN I SHARE MY HOBBIES WITH FRIENDS AND TURN THEM INTO ENJOYABLE
SOCIAL ACTIVITIES THAT STRENGTHEN OUR CONNECTIONS?

All the questions are available in a separate bonus file (link provided at the beginning of the book). So, no worries about cutting!

"Success is getting what you want,
happiness is wanting what you get"
— W.P. Kinsella

YOU
DESERVE
TO BE
HAPPY

SUCCESS

YES
you can

2025

EXCUSES
ARE USELESS
RESULTS
ARE PRICELESS

IF YOU
NEVER TRY,
YOU WILL
NEVER KNOW

FOCUS ON
BEING PRODUCTIVE
INSTEAD OF BUSY

Learning & Self-Development

1

DO I HAVE ANY GLOBAL EDUCATIONAL GOALS, SUCH AS EARNING A DEGREE OR COMPLETING A CERTIFICATION, AND WHAT ACTIONABLE STEPS DO I PLAN TO TAKE TO PURSUE THESE GOALS?

2

WHAT NEW SKILLS OR KNOWLEDGE HAVE I GAINED IN THE PAST YEAR, AND HOW HAVE THEY BENEFITED ME?

3

WHAT AREAS OF MY LIFE DO I WANT TO GROW IN, AND WHAT STEPS CAN I TAKE TO DEVELOP THOSE SKILLS?

4

HOW CAN I INCORPORATE CONTINUOUS LEARNING INTO MY DAILY ROUTINE?

5

AM I ACTIVELY SEEKING OPPORTUNITIES FOR PERSONAL GROWTH?

6

HOW DO I STAY MOTIVATED TO PURSUE SELF-DEVELOPMENT?

7

WHAT SUBJECTS OR SKILLS EXCITE ME MOST, AND HOW CAN I EXPLORE THEM FURTHER?

8

HOW DO I MEASURE PROGRESS IN MY PERSONAL GROWTH JOURNEY?

9

ARE THERE MENTORS OR RESOURCES I CAN TURN TO FOR GUIDANCE IN MY SELF-DEVELOPMENT?

10

WHAT HABITS OR ROUTINES CAN I ESTABLIS TO PRIORITIZE LIFELONG LEARNING?

All the questions are available in a separate bonus file (link provided at the beginning of the book). So, no worries about cutting!

"Invest in yourself. It pays the best interest"

INVEST *in* KNOWLEDGE

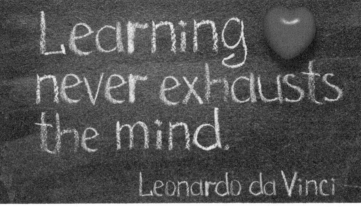

Learning never exhausts the mind.

Leonardo da Vinci

BILINGUAL

~~UNEMPLOYED~~
~~UNWANTED~~
~~UNSKILLED~~

Career & Financial Growth

1

WHAT CAREER ACHIEVEMENTS HAVE I ACCOMPLISHED IN THE PAST YEAR,
AND HOW DO THEY ALIGN WITH MY LONG-TERM GOALS?

2

AM I SATISFIED WITH MY CURRENT CAREER PATH, OR DO I FEEL THE NEED
FOR CHANGE OR ADVANCEMENT?

3

WHAT SKILLS DO I NEED TO ACQUIRE OR IMPROVE TO ADVANCE
IN MY CAREER?

4

HOW CAN I CREATE MORE FINANCIAL STABILITY AND GROWTH IN MY LIFE?

5

WHAT IS MY LONG-TERM FINANCIAL GOAL, AND AM I ON TRACK TO ACHIEVE IT?

6

HOW EFFECTIVELY DO I MANAGE MY INCOME AND SAVINGS?

7

AM I TAKING ADVANTAGE OF OPPORTUNITIES FOR CAREER DEVELOPMENT,
SUCH AS TRAINING OR MENTORSHIP?

8

HOW CAN I IMPROVE MY WORK-LIFE BALANCE TO MAINTAIN BOTH CAREER
SUCCESS AND PERSONAL WELL-BEING?

9

WHAT STEPS CAN I TAKE TO INCREASE MY EARNING POTENTIAL
IN THE COMING YEAR?

10

HOW DOES MY CURRENT CAREER ALIGN WITH MY PERSONAL VALUES
AND PASSIONS, AND WHAT CHANGES CAN I MAKE TO BRING THEM INTO
ALIGNMENT?

*All the questions are available in a separate bonus file (link provided at the
beginning of the book). So, no worries about cutting!*

I am a
POWERFUL
MONEY
MAGNET

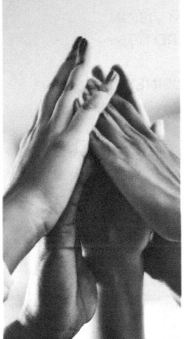

BELIEVING
IN YOURSELF
IS THE FIRST SECRET
TO SUCCESS

Business & Investments

1

DO I WANT AND DO I FEEL READY TO START MY OWN BUSINESS,
AND WHAT STEPS CAN I TAKE TO MAKE THIS SHIFT?

2

WHAT TYPE OF BUSINESS ALIGNS WITH MY PASSIONS, SKILLS,
AND LONG-TERM GOALS, AND WHY DOES THIS VENTURE EXCITE ME?

3

WHAT STEPS CAN I TAKE TO TRANSITION FROM THINKING ABOUT STARTING
A BUSINESS TO TAKING ACTIONABLE STEPS TOWARD LAUNCHING IT?

4

IF I HAVE BUSINESS ALREADY, WHAT IS THE LONG-TERM VISION
FOR MY BUSINESS, AND HOW AM I WORKING TOWARD IT?

5

WHAT STEPS CAN I TAKE TO EXPAND OR SCALE MY BUSINESS
IN THE NEXT YEAR?

6

HOW DOES MY BUSINESS ALIGN WITH MY PERSONAL VALUES AND GOALS?

7

WHAT CHALLENGES HAVE I FACED IN MY BUSINESS,
AND HOW CAN I OVERCOME THEM?

8

HOW CAN I INCREASE REVENUE STREAMS?

9

AM I INVESTING IN MY PROFESSIONAL GROWTH,
AND WHAT MORE CAN I DO?

10

DO I WANT TO MAKE SMART INVESTMENTS THAT ALIGN WITH MY LONG-TERM
FINANCIAL GOALS, AND WHAT DO I NEED TO LEARN OR RESEARCH TO MOVE
FORWARD IN THIS DIRECTION?

All the questions are available in a separate bonus file (link provided at the beginning of the book). So, no worries about cutting!

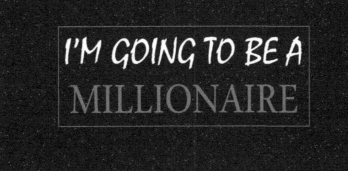

I'M GOING TO BE A

MILLIONAIRE

WORK SMART NOT HARD

#

MAKE MONEY WHILE YOU SLEEP

REFLECTIVE QUESTIONS
Digital Presence & Goals

1
WHAT DO I WANT MY ONLINE PRESENCE TO REPRESENT ABOUT ME,
AND HOW CAN I ALIGN IT WITH MY PERSONAL VALUES?

2
HOW CAN I USE MY ONLINE PLATFORM TO SHARE MY PASSIONS, SKILLS,
OR EXPERIENCES WITH A WIDER AUDIENCE?

3
WHAT TYPE OF CONTENT DO I ENJOY CREATING,
AND HOW CAN I STAY CONSISTENT WITH SHARING IT?

4
HOW CAN I LEVERAGE SOCIAL MEDIA TO CONNECT WITH LIKE-MINDED INDIVIDUALS
AND GROW MY PERSONAL NETWORK?

5
WHAT PERSONAL STRENGTHS OR UNIQUE PERSPECTIVES CAN I HIGHLIGHT
TO DIFFERENTIATE MYSELF ONLINE?

6
WHAT GOALS DO I HAVE FOR GROWING MY SELF-BRAND,
AND HOW CAN I MEASURE PROGRESS OVER TIME?

7
HOW CAN I MAKE MY ONLINE PRESENCE FEEL AUTHENTIC
WHILE STILL ENGAGING MY AUDIENCE?

8
WHAT PLATFORMS BEST SUIT MY SELF-BRAND,
AND HOW CAN I MAXIMIZE THEIR POTENTIAL?

9
WHAT STEPS CAN I TAKE TO BUILD CONFIDENCE IN PUTTING MYSELF
OUT THERE ONLINE?

10
HOW CAN I ENSURE THAT MY ONLINE PRESENCE REFLECTS THE PERSON
I WANT TO BECOME?

All the questions are available in a separate bonus file (link provided at the beginning of the book). So, no worries about cutting!

MAKE
MONEY
ONLINE

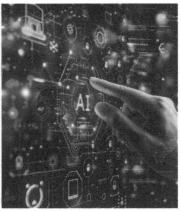

KNOW YOUR WORTH

ROYALTIES

THANK YOU
10K
FOLLOWERS

Luxury Lifestyle

1
WHAT DOES LIVING A LUXURY LIFESTYLE MEAN TO ME,
AND HOW DOES IT ALIGN WITH MY PERSONAL VALUES?

2
WHAT SPECIFIC LUXURY EXPERIENCES OR ITEMS DO I DESIRE,
AND WHY ARE THEY IMPORTANT TO ME?

3
HOW CAN I ACHIEVE A BALANCE BETWEEN PURSUING LUXURY
AND MAINTAINING FINANCIAL STABILITY?

4
WHAT STEPS CAN I TAKE TO BRING MORE LUXURY
INTO MY EVERYDAY LIFE WITHOUT OVERSPENDING?

5
HOW DO I ENVISION ENJOYING THE BENEFITS OF A LUXURY LIFESTYLE
WHILE REMAINING GROUNDED AND FULFILLED?

All the questions are available in a separate bonus file (link provided at the beginning of the book). So, no worries about cutting!

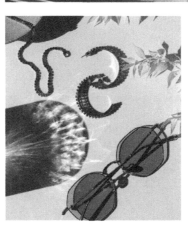

"Being rich is having money;
being wealthy is having time."
— Margaret Bonanno

BOARDING PASS

VIP TICKET

NAME:

DATE: TIME:

DESTINATION:

NAME:

DESTINATION:

DATE:

FLIGHT CLASS:

BOARDING PASS

VIP TICKET

NAME:

DATE: TIME:

DESTINATION:

NAME:

DESTINATION:

DATE:

FLIGHT CLASS:

BANK OF THE UNIVERSE

0001

DATE: _____

$

PAY TO THE
ORDER OF: _____

_____ DOLLARS 🔒

NOTE: _____   SIGNATURE _____

1234567890   12345678   1234

BANK OF THE UNIVERSE

0001

DATE: _____

$

PAY TO THE
ORDER OF: _____

_____ DOLLARS 🔒

NOTE: _____   SIGNATURE _____

1234567890   12345678   1234

REFLECTIVE QUESTIONS

Travel & Adventures

1
WHAT TYPES OF TRAVEL EXPERIENCES EXCITE ME THE MOST,
AND HOW CAN I PLAN TO EXPLORE MORE OF THEM?

2
HOW DO MY TRAVEL GOALS ALIGN WITH MY PERSONAL VALUES,
SUCH AS ADVENTURE, RELAXATION, OR CULTURAL EXPLORATION?

3
WHAT DESTINATIONS HAVE I ALWAYS DREAMED OF VISITING,
AND WHAT STEPS CAN I TAKE TO MAKE THOSE TRIPS A REALITY?

4
HOW DO I BALANCE TRAVEL AND ADVENTURE WITH MY OTHER
RESPONSIBILITIES, AND HOW CAN I PRIORITIZE MORE TIME FOR
EXPLORATION?

5
HOW CAN I CREATE MEANINGFUL TRAVEL EXPERIENCES THAT
I CAN SHARE AND CHERISH WITH MY LOVED ONES, DEEPENING
OUR CONNECTION THROUGH SHARED ADVENTURES?

*All the questions are available in a separate bonus file (link provided at the
beginning of the book). So, no worries about cutting!*

On the next page:

London, UK
Athens, Greece
Barcelona, Spain
Amsterdam, Netherlands
Lisbon, Portugal
Venice, Italy
Tokyo, Japan
Paris, France

"The most beautiful in the world is, of course, the world itself."
— Wallace Stevens

On the next page:

Dubai, UAE
Berlin, Germany
Singapore, Singapore
Vienna, Austria
Las Vegas, USA
Rome, Italy
Copenhagen, Denmark
Sydney, Australia
Saint Petersburg, Russia

"Collect moments, not things."
— Unknown

"If you think you can, you can.
And if you think you can't, you're right."
— Henry Ford

SAVING
MONEY

INVEST

BINGO !

YOUR
MINDSET
IS WHAT
WILL
MAKE
YOU
A MILLIONAIRE.

I have not failed.
I've just found 10,000 ways
that won't work.

"
Hold the
vision, trust
the process.

BELIEVE
YOU CAN
and you're
HALFWAY THERE

PASSIVE

INCOME

Me-Time & Self-Care

1

HOW OFTEN DO I MAKE TIME FOR MYSELF, AND IS IT ENOUGH
TO RECHARGE AND REFRESH?

2

WHAT ACTIVITIES MAKE ME FEEL MOST RELAXED
AND REJUVENATED, AND HOW CAN I INCORPORATE
THEM MORE REGULARLY?

3

AM I SETTING HEALTHY BOUNDARIES TO PROTECT MY PERSONAL
TIME AND WELL-BEING?

4

HOW CAN I BETTER PRIORITIZE SELF-CARE WITHOUT FEELING GUILTY
OR OVERWHELMED?

5

WHAT SMALL DAILY RITUALS CAN I CREATE TO NURTURE
MY MENTAL, EMOTIONAL, AND PHYSICAL HEALTH?

All the questions are available in a separate bonus file (link provided at the beginning of the book). So, no worries about cutting!

TAKE CARE
OF
YOURSELF

STOP

Mindfulness & Gratitude

1

HOW OFTEN DO I TAKE TIME TO BE FULLY PRESENT IN THE MOMENT, AND HOW DOES IT AFFECT MY OVERALL WELL-BEING?

2

WHAT PRACTICES OR ACTIVITIES HELP ME STAY MINDFUL,
AND HOW CAN I INCORPORATE THEM MORE CONSISTENTLY INTO MY DAILY ROUTINE?

3

IN WHAT AREAS OF MY LIFE DO I TEND TO BE THE LEAST MINDFUL,
AND HOW CAN I IMPROVE MY AWARENESS IN THOSE MOMENTS?

4

HOW DO I HANDLE STRESS, AND HOW CAN MINDFULNESS HELP ME RESPOND TO CHALLENGES WITH GREATER CALM AND CLARITY?

5

WHAT BENEFITS HAVE I EXPERIENCED FROM MINDFULNESS,
AND HOW CAN I DEEPEN MY PRACTICE FOR FURTHER PERSONAL GROWTH?

6

HOW OFTEN DO I TAKE TIME TO ACKNOWLEDGE AND APPRECIATE
THE THINGS I'M GRATEFUL FOR IN MY LIFE?

7

IN WHAT WAYS HAS PRACTICING GRATITUDE IMPROVED MY OUTLOOK
OR RELATIONSHIPS, AND HOW CAN I DEEPEN THIS PRACTICE?

8

WHAT SPECIFIC MOMENTS OR PEOPLE AM I MOST THANKFUL FOR,
AND HOW CAN I EXPRESS THAT GRATITUDE MORE REGULARLY?

All the questions are available in a separate bonus file (link provided at the beginning of the book). So, no worries about cutting!

Mind
Body
Soul

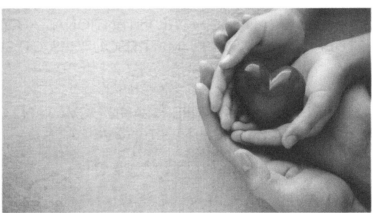

Mindful
living

THANKFUL
GRATEFUL
BLESSED

REFLECTIVE QUESTIONS
Kindness & Giving

1
HOW OFTEN DO I PRACTICE ACTS OF KINDNESS,
AND HOW DO THESE ACTIONS IMPACT MY SENSE OF FULFILLMENT?

2
IN WHAT WAYS CAN I BE MORE INTENTIONAL ABOUT GIVING,
WHETHER THROUGH MY TIME, RESOURCES, OR SUPPORT?

3
HOW DO I FEEL WHEN I HELP OTHERS, AND HOW CAN I CULTIVATE MORE
OPPORTUNITIES TO GIVE BACK?

4
ARE THERE AREAS IN MY LIFE WHERE I CAN SHOW MORE KINDNESS,
BOTH TO MYSELF AND THOSE AROUND ME?

5
WHAT CAUSES OR COMMUNITIES AM I PASSIONATE ABOUT,
AND HOW CAN I CONTRIBUTE TO THEM IN A MEANINGFUL WAY?

All the questions are available in a separate bonus file (link provided at the beginning of the book). So, no worries about cutting!

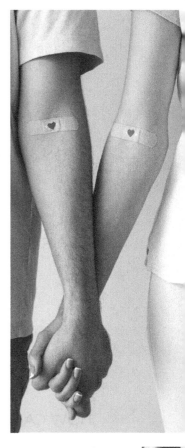

TOGETHER WE MAKE THE DIFFERENCE

WE RISE BY LIFTING OTHERS

Give

GIVING

DONATE

REFLECTIVE QUESTIONS
Me & My Planet

1

HOW CONSCIOUS AM I OF MY DAILY HABITS AND THEIR IMPACT
ON THE ENVIRONMENT, AND WHAT CHANGES CAN I MAKE TO REDUCE
MY FOOTPRINT?

2

WHAT STEPS AM I CURRENTLY TAKING TO LIVE A MORE SUSTAINABLE LIFESTYLE,
AND HOW CAN I IMPROVE MY EFFORTS?

3

IN WHAT WAYS CAN I BETTER CONTRIBUTE TO THE PRESERVATION
AND PROTECTION OF NATURAL RESOURCES?

4

HOW CAN I INCORPORATE ECO-FRIENDLY PRACTICES INTO MY HOME, WORK,
AND COMMUNITY LIFE?

5

WHAT SPECIFIC ACTIONS CAN I TAKE TO SUPPORT ENVIRONMENTAL CAUSES
OR INITIATIVES THAT ALIGN WITH MY VALUES?

All the questions are available in a separate bonus file (link provided at the beginning of the book). So, no worries about cutting!

REDUCE
REUSE
RECYCLE
REPEAT

PROTECT
OUR
PLANET

LESS
IS
MORE

QUALITY,
NOT QUANTITY

There is

no

planet B

"In the middle of every difficulty lies opportunity."
— Albert Einstein

choose happy

DO MORE OF WHAT MAKES YOU HAPPY

BE KIND TO YOUR •SELF•

GRATITUDE CHANGES EVERYTHING

"The best way to predict your future is to create it."
— Abraham Lincoln

I CAN AND I WILL

Watch me.

1 YEAR

=

365 OPPORTUNITIES

GOOD VIBES ONLY

BREATHE DEEP

ENJOY LIFE

YESTERDAY IS GONE.
TOMORROW HAS NOT YET COME.
WE HAVE ONLY TODAY.
LET US BEGIN.

WHEN WAS THE
LAST TIME
YOU DID SOMETHING
FOR THE FIRST
TIME ?

BIG JOURNEYS

BEGIN WITH

SMALL STEPS

LOVE MORE.

READ MORE.

WRITE MORE.

DREAM MORE.

LIVE MORE.

Setting goals
is the first
STEP IN TURNING
THE INVISIBLE
into the
visible.

IF YOU DREAM IT, YOU CAN DO it

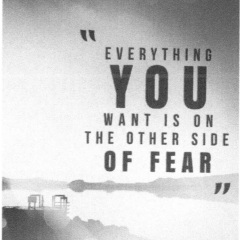

"
EVERYTHING
YOU
WANT IS ON
THE OTHER SIDE
OF FEAR
"

THE BEST WAY
TO PREDICT
THE FUTURE IS TO
CREATE IT.

"Whatever you do, or dream you can do, begin it. Boldness has genius, power and magic in it."
— Johann Wolfgang Von Goethe

DON'T LET THE NOISE OF OTHERS' OPINIONS DROWN OUT YOUR OWN INNER VOICE.

DON'T STOP UNTIL YOU ARE PROUD.

Do it now.
SOMETIMES 'LATER' BECOMES 'NEVER'

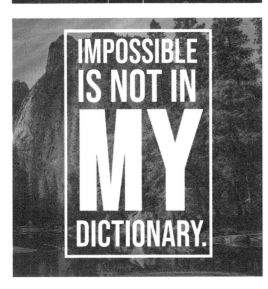

IMPOSSIBLE IS NOT IN MY DICTIONARY.

Forget the **MISTAKE.** **REMEMBER** *the lesson*

EVER TRIED. EVER FAILED. NO MATTER. TRY AGAIN. FAIL AGAIN. FAIL BETTER.

I EMBRACE THE RESPONSIBILITIES THAT COME WITH WEALTH AND USE IT TO MAKE A POSITIVE IMPACT ON THE WORLD.

ASK YOURSELF IF WHAT YOU ARE DOING TODAY IS GETTING YOU CLOSER TO WHERE YOU WANT TO BE TOMORROW.

DREAM BIG, WORK HARD, STAY FOCUSED AND SURROUND YOURSELF WITH GOOD PEOPLE.

WHEN THE VISION IS CLEAR, STRATEGY IS EASY

ACCEPT NO ONE'S DEFINITION OF YOUR LIFE, DEFINE YOURSELF."

GO CONFIDENTLY IN THE DIRECTION OF YOUR DREAMS, LIVE THE LIFE YOU HAVE IMAGINED

"Many of life's failures are people who did not realize how close they were to success when they gave up."
— Thomas A. Edison

I am dedicated, focused and ready to succeed in my career or business plans.

Opportunities for growth and success are always coming my way.

I attract success by being my authentic self.

Every day, I am becoming healthier and more balanced.

My body is vibrant and resilient, and I treat it with care and respect.

I am healthy, strong and full of energy.

I attract love, kindness and understanding into all of my relationships.

I am worthy of deep and meaningful connections.

I am surrounded by love and I bring out the best in others.

My relationships are filled with mutual respect, trust and affection.

I love & I am loved.

I give and receive love effortlessly.

I am financially secure and I attract wealth and prosperity.

I make smart financial decisions that lead to growth and success.

Money flows to me easily and effortlessly.

I am constantly growing and becoming the best version of myself.

I trust the process of life and allow myself to evolve.

I am capable of achieving anything I set my mind to.

"Chance favors the prepared mind."
— Louis Pasteur

FOLLOW YOUR HEART

Balance

BE THE TYPE OF PERSON YOU WANT TO MEET

WORK from HOME

YOU CAN DO ANYTHING

Eat less sugar, you're sweet enough already

10M LIKES

I AM HEALTHY

I AM FINANCIALLY ABUNDANT

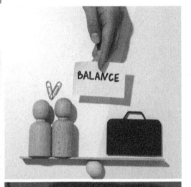
BALANCE

KEEP GOING
KEEP GOING
KEEP GOING
KEEP GOING
KEEP GOING
KEEP GOING

namaste

START each day with a Grateful HEART

IT'S A GOOD DAY TO HAVE A GOOD DAY

Sleep WELL

I REMAIN HUMBLE AND GROUNDED DESPITE MY NEWFOUND FORTUNE.

DO ALL THINGS WITH LOVE

DRINK MORE WATER

LEARN JAPANESE

LEARN ITALIAN

I am rich IN ALL AREAS OF MY LIFE

BLOGGIN' QUEEN

"You don't have to be great to start,
but you have to start to be great."
— Zig Ziglar

Mutual Love	Constant Support	High Productivity
Total Harmony	Self-Love	Mutual Trust
Close Connection	Full Understanding	Happy Family
Fiery Passion	Endless Energy	Perfect Unity
Open Sexuality	Healthy Balance	Physical Wellness
Inner Peace	Calm Focus	Present Awareness
Self-Care	Relaxing Escape	Social Success
Career Success	Job Promotion	Salary Increase
Strong Leadership	Business Start Up	Great Wealth
Creative Solutions	New Opportunities	Dream Car
Strong Motivation	Dream Home	Driven Ambition
Endless Luck	Public Recognition	Global Expansion

"Vision with action can change the world."
— J. A. Baker

"Yesterday is history. Tomorrow is a mystery.
Today is a gift. That's why we call it The Present."
— Bil Keane

BE BOLD!

BE YOU!

2025

I WILL DO BIG THINGS.

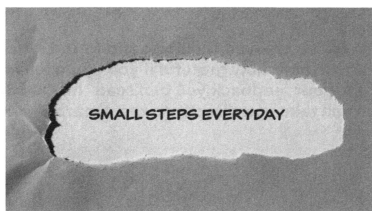

SMALL STEPS EVERYDAY

YOU ALWAYS HAVE A CHOICE

CHOOSE TO BE HAPPY

CREATE A LIFE YOU DON'T NEED A VACATION FROM

Thank You!

I want to sincerely thank you for choosing this book
to accompany you on your journey of dream manifestation.
I hope the images, affirmations, and tips within these pages have sparked
inspiration and excitement as you work toward your goals.

Remember, every small step brings you closer to your dreams.
Stay consistent, keep believing in the power of your vision,
and.. trust the process!

**If you've enjoyed the book and found it helpful,
I would be incredibly grateful if you could leave a review.
To share your feedback you can scan the QR code below,
which will take you directly to the Amazon review page.**

Wishing you great success and joy
in bringing your dreams to life!

With gratitude,
Lisa Sinclair
Mindful Vision Press